The Names

books by **Tim Lilburn**

poetry
Names of God (1986)
Tourist to Ecstasy (1989)
From the Great Above She Opened Her Ear to the Great Below
(with Susan Shantz) (1991)
Moosewood Sandhills (1994)
To the River (1999)
Kill-site (2003)
Desire Never Leaves: The Poetry of Tim Lilburn
(with Alison Calder) (2006)
Orphic Politics (2008)
Assiniboia (2012)
The Names (2016)

essays
Poetry and Knowing: Speculative Essays and Interviews (editor) (1995)
Living in the World As If It Were Home (1999)
Thinking and Singing: Poetry and the Practice of Philosophy (editor) (2002)
Going Home: Essays (2008)

Tim Lilburn **The Names**

McClelland & Stewart

Copyright © 2016 by Tim Lilburn

All rights reserved. The use of any part of this publication reproduced, transmitted in any form or by any means, electronic, mechanical, photocopying, recording, or otherwise, or stored in a retrieval system, without the prior written consent of the publisher – or, in case of photocopying or other reprographic copying, a licence from the Canadian Copyright Licensing Agency – is an infringement of the copyright law.

Library and Archives Canada Cataloguing in Publication

Lilburn, Tim, 1950-, author
    The names / Tim Lilburn.

Poems.
Issued in print and electronic formats.
ISBN 978-0-7710-4803-6 (paperback). – ISBN 978-0-7710-4804-3 (epub)

    I. Title.

PS8573.I427N34 2016   C811'.54   C2015-907698-6
                                                                                    C2015-907699-4

Published simultaneously in the United States of America by McClelland & Stewart, a division of Random House of Canada Limited, a Penguin Random House Company

Library of Congress Control Number is available upon request

Cover design by Five Seventeen
Cover art: © Igor Madjinca / Stocksy
Typeset in Baskerville by M&S, Toronto
Printed and bound in the USA

McClelland & Stewart, a division of Random House of Canada Limited, a Penguin Random House Company
www.penguinrandomhouse.ca

1 2 3 4 5   20 19 18 17 16

The Real willed, glorified be He, in virtue of His Beautiful Names, which are innumerable, to see their identities – if you wish to say: to see His Identity – in a comprehensive being that comprises the whole affair insofar as it is possessed of existence, and His Mystery is manifest to Himself through it.

Ibn 'Arabi, *Fusus al-hikam*

Contents

I
Aunt Mary   1
Beauty Wall   2
West Slope, Sooke Hills   3
The Marian River, Milan   4
January 8, 2014: *De more*   6
Theodosia   7
Republic   8
Rosemont   9
Ricardo   12
The Northern City   13
The Barracks, 1954   16
Of   17

II
Sara Riel, the Convent, Île-à-la-Crosse, 1874   21
End of August   23
Swan Plain   24
Oh   25
Tim Lilburn the trained Jesuit seal has for years etc.   26
Fucked Up, All Fucked Up   27
Magnus es, Domine, et laudabilis valde (Augustine, *Confessions*)   29
Exempla   30
Black Hut   32
Rabbit Lake Log House, Where I First Read the *Tao*   33
Nature   34

III
The Munroe Wing   39
The Fifties   40
Deer Place Hut   42
That Time   43
Poem Coming to Ruusbroec   45
Summer, 1971   48
The Leighton Ford Crusade, Regina Exhibition Stadium, 1962   49

IV
Rivers and Mountains in the Mouth of the Exegetical Choir   53
Retreat   55
Feast   56
Against "Linguistic Fragmentation as Political Intervention in Calgarian Poetry," derek beaulieu, *Open Letter*, Summer, 2008   57
P,KOLS Song Cycle   60
Mountain   65

Notes and Acknowledgements   67

Aunt Mary

A black-handled jackknife
Left in a steamer trunk, Glaswegian troll,
Tight with coin, George Hendy, 5' 4",
Is knocking at the bottom
Of steep basement stairs.
Janitor, four to midnight,
At Imperial Oil in the city's northeast cindery snow,
He pilfered milky letterhead, which he slipped to my father,
Who fed it to me, and squirrelled away one hundred thousand dollars
From pieces of string and empty coffee cans
Put to arcane use and willed it
To his son, care of the King's Hotel's
Fire and Shadow Lounge.
Badly knapped tongue, mesomorphic stealth
On a short track, tellurian, garden sewn in gravel,
Small wheat of the man. Only sanctity
On protestant campaign rations
Could live with that – Aunt Mary's scored face
Swivelling adoration to my brother and me.
She, from syrup of Dromore dirt,
Pulled through a marriage's needle eye
Grew skinned in her wits, and what that did to her language
Was a forest she crossed in the end,
Leaving.
I see her shoot through my mother's screen door,
Hours after supper, some fall in the Seventies,
Nattering a private grasshopper lingo,
Douglas fir on the back of her Siwash sweater swaying,
George up and after on bad hips.

Beauty Wall

The fault rolls on bearings of water
Beneath Vancouver Island.
A rope of knotted hymns, I rappel down,
My toes touch the feldspar-lumened floor.
As I move, testing and palming the slow-turning sacks
               I find a pile of old clothes.
Here are Sara Riel's letters
Rolled and jammed into the toe of a shoe,
I pick them up and read.
At the end of one are directions to a jewel-blistered exegesis
On the Gospel of St. John, upon which I also dine,
Where is said only the noun
Has no weight
Slide from it.
Only the noun remains to cook the evening meal.

West Slope, Sooke Hills

Snow, then clear-cut
In slanting, wavy rectangles, creek
Gashes under shifting cloud
Colour of a robin's back,
Then a two-track groove
Falling through solid green, Oregon
Grape as you follow it, ratty broom
Like shitted turkey tail
Until cranberry bogs, blackberries, tidal pools,
Farthest out stones clacking in sea pull.
I thought I could meet her again, her still keeping herself
Company, that soft clickety-click speech, back and forth,
A baby raccoon warm inside her clothes,
In her body-length apron and seamed hose,
Coming down one of these deactivated
Mains over rain-greased rocks
In brogues or nearly erased Eaton slippers.
Her shy, removable, new-salmon smile – *she's* amused,
By the spreading field-thing, a bit off
The ground,
That's tracked and, pulse-bag, holds her, Mary, to breathe for her,
But she's ready for the likelihood I will not have taken this in
And could be embarrassed by the drunken recognition
Saturating her face.

The Marian River, Milan

Snow slabs in the dicey cedar hedge,
    robins and winter wrens thickly
        inside, taking stick from the cold.
One wren looks to plant a nest in the shed's roof
and moves around the complete structure below the overhang,
feet pinging on anti-raccoon wire.
Moan of the weather. What does it mean?
The shed backs into a half-acre of maples and fir,
which joins an oak sprawl beside a cliff at the west side –
                my body – of a rounded horn mountain.
In summer there's a cosmological map gold lichen spread on cliff stone
behind a punji cluster of blackberries.
The pear tree at the window facing the mountain – one May a rubythroated
hummingbird sat weeks on two bean-sized eggs
in a moss and succulent nest, at eye height,
armed, pointed flame,

equal to or exceeding Augustine in Milan
and later in Hippo, where he writes to Atticus, patriarch of Constantinople,
three times in 421, definitively, on sexuality, "on which he had meditated for
    over two decades"
and hears nothing. Dusty, now in his sixties, buried in the rural stone.
Atticus holds stories he is dead,
he reasons, true.

Winds swim under rock on the mountain,
flowing down, each with its own face.
A muscularity of breath, feathering.
My seven-skeletoned name
makes out the smell,

faces, each a scent
and a name also. So I come toward the winds,
clean but with no disinterrable docking mechanism for them.

But he is not dead. Rather he sits in Hippo,
later called Annaba, which is pretty and hick on the wrong side of *mare nostrum*
and which will wait six hundred years for thonged Italian and French tourists
to come and harvest air,
just as Mousterians waited in this cove for homo sapiens to claim
their beach space with geometric thought. He waits for his letter, barely
caught in the imperial swell,
his foot nevertheless on the Donatist neck,
Rome north and above him glittering, a universal Turing machine
in which anything could happen.
Leave him. Roughly nothing will come of this.
Marx will work out the small epicyclic gear structure
operating the whole affair later. History
rolls forward
on treads that are rivers, the river-system perhaps of Mary,
these rivers, the colourless, alkaline lymph of the world, idea's
body.

January 8, 2014: *De more*

Owls in back firs, rain basaltic,
sheer, briefly cut
after weeks, feast of Nazianzus and Basil the Great,
warriors in glimmering
dragon skin platting, Nicea's
fighters, just gone, Arians, their perfumed
faces, nevertheless still everywhere,
mouthing hummingbird clicks
        at the emperor's elbow, breathing on the golden sleeve.
Thus tankers slide into the Strait.
Venus is an eruption in the unlightening west.
Slowly roof frost appears,
white slabs breaking down to Shelbourne St.
and the line I've grooved on asphalt
with my eye for Bowker Creek
in its unringing culvert.
Everyone who thinks must shake.

Theodosia

There you are. A photograph of wind,
Ireland, 1923. The other sister.
The face a winged stone, the rest of you
Anchor-snagged in funeral meringue of 1897 clothes,
Your brothers, knee-shorted, lost
As blown dirt.
Towns south Patrick Kavanagh
Moves, parting cow stink
With a widow's peak
A foot below the spines.
One leg in front of the other, slightly bent,
Commando pose, the fleet, detonated stare,
You are taller than Hughie and my father, in mid-flight,
Red hair, in travelling windrows,
Casual and wrecking as Viking raids.

Air above the yellow-brown couch
Cliffy with Players, fifty years later;
The whomp and chop of your laugh
Settles everything. North Regina, December,
I'm back for a few days,
A bottle is tucked like a letter for me always
Between cushions.
Unread, gaga for argument, comical wolverine,
A New Model Army of moods on manoeuvres
In your hilltribes Quaker heart, the speed of you
Coming from the bow, whistling, bright,
Merciless, besotted.

Republic

The creek was corrupt and
put us in itself
in one of its smooth, octagonal cells.
Ten steps across,
a brown fish, large, in it that we killed.
The creek a black ledger
where our
names fell as sediment.
We made a way through weeds
                      down a slope,
leaping white
concrete chunks breaching from it,
the air mostly peppery arc-welding bloom.
The creek was a horned ring
that when it hit us left a
tattoo.
We, instantly one, signed up.
We sank.
We smelled of muskrats immediately.
Our eyes under the water
grew solid dark.
My brother, my eyes, the Pelletier girls and John.
We turned to one another as algae globs
bloated and deflected past us in the flow.

Rosemont

     1
I float over propane tanks, back lanes,
outhouses in pyjamas, twelve, over shacks and the more-
than-shacks, north of trolley wires and an edge of the city
forest. I drift just above the tips of elms, and am twelve. June.
People are asleep below, the milkman's
horse waits on Connaught for the man to come through
a lilac hedge, marsupial pouch
first, empties percussing in his iron basket.
Someone, Yvonne I guess, the Pelletiers' oldest,
sets kindling to take off the chill.
The horse is motionless above its cake-sized,
cement anchor.

The man next door comes onto his back step and lowers
a match into a pipe bowl, a perfect 1938 maroon Chevrolet
sedan parked, never driven, in his garage, and the woman, Mrs. Garvin,
farther down walks into her irises as John Pelletier loads
the family wash tub on the wagon
and goes for water.

     2
Wilfrid carried a straight razor he
shortened with a file
        to flick easier.
More operatic, chthonic device than the Hollywood
switchblade Charlie Crow, Jimmy South's psychotic cousin,
drew from an anklelength black coat,
to rob my brother of chips and a Fanta orange
outside Moon's Confectionary. Kryptonited
by ideology, Charlie'd still slice.

But a shotgun was Wilf's true, later wonder
instrument, his completer
of aesthetic shape. There it was
in his hand in the 2:00 a.m. nightclub, under the stream-surface
ball, a wakening deep in the cave. Lucky we didn't go
to Martin, says my brother. Be in jail now.
Or out, superannuated, blinking,
our eyes fondling a range of knots.
Bob Cooke, the Gland, in the giant lobby
of the hotel, twenty-one, handgunned,
tendoned stillness hatched around him,
a single counter-tenor note held,
held, just now starting to fade, lose ground
and fade, that emotion-sound, now
cranes his neck forward and asks
the night-clerk to open the safe,
wide the door to the ivied grotto in the wall,
ovoid hole the animal's body made
in the mat of low bushes by passing in and out.

3

> *"delectable absorption"*
> St. Teresa of Avila

The eatable world leans against us,
                neuronal pathways, beauty sheen,
fish clouds bulging walls,
tympanic throb of reindeer
narrowing through gorges.
I put my hand, quite a while ago, years ago
actually onto the knee of the Fish-Lord
                and individuality appeared.
There was no pain.

Those days when I sat in that room
in Osprey Cabins, rain chipping
the window, I would rise
to kneel and set my ear to the floor.
I heard most of what occurred.
Those days left almost all of their firepits in me.
                    I say hello.
The gorgeous wave,
metaphysics chrismed with chlorophyll and skin,
lifts midway through the body, near the waist, and rolls
                    through.

        4
I am asleep and drift over the neighbourhood,
grazing carragana leaves, elm leaves.
There's the creek, two miles away, then beyond
behind cattails, the RCMP Training Depot and almost
beneath me now that I've crossed over
Dewdney Ave., the turret and chimneys
of the Lieutenant Governor's residence now empty,
except for aspirate or soul carapaces
of the dead we can see clearly through dusty groundfloor windows.
A muskrat's splitting the surface of the creek and John,
returning, sheds rim splashes
on the wood sidewalk. Behind him,
now that he's turned into Connaught
and has the wagon at the back door, water swaying,
the first trolley bus sparks and rattles toward downtown
and I am settling, descended through the scorch
from overhead wires, unseen, barefoot,
upright, on my parents' lawn.

Ricardo

He's made a bed for himself
in the room of a long kitchen knife
or he sinks into a stream,
understream slide, where as he sharpens, clarity
pinholes him between the eyes. He hears applause
of a paid-for
smacking, arriving in his breast, he deliverer
of the goods, his name on the cheque,
he's genuine smoke, the uranium gun.
He places his throat in material fervour.
He bobs in the flow of Rilke's queer Christology,
chaotic bumping of carnivorous perfections.
He pours all muscle into a spire
resting on a single, simple x.
Movement in his chest and arms,
horses quickly circling.

The Northern City

Richard assembled out of a blizzard
He'd come south inside down the Nelson River
And was before a cup of scabby tea in box canyon
Of fluorescent jerk.
Richard enjarred me in eyes flicked
From two wolves, one blue, one grey,
In the starving, balled-up light of the Ideal Tea Room,
Jim the Chinese owner drifting behind the counter,
Richard with ribs-showing tea.
After supper, the front part of the store
Was wet cardboard, ice decayed
From shoes, weak cooking out of the back
From behind the cloth sewn around a wire.
Richard sat on a twirly stool, the blizzard he came in
Denned inside his coat.
Richard-Ogun, grains of iron
Sequestered throughout his body,
Richard-the-Sturgeon,
About to gather for a possible kicking
Or an ascension under the dash
In a stranger's car, twiddling wires.
Winter outside, thirty below, wolves
On the cement, chipping at what was left.
Richard has curtained me in his eyes.
I talk to him, I keep talking and what
I send toward his face drains away from the surface.
To him, I was lifting tiny, chaffed stones
From the crop wattling below his chin,
He believed he caught me translating his tailfeathers
Into American dollars.
Richard-Grendl. He moves his head

As if he'd received a faraway, go-to-able smell baking off me. His head moves,
Neck extended, but thinks no, no, and drops me.

His theatrical body swimming above
His real one, Richard-White-Whale, Richard
Burning under the ground, hole-in-the-water,
Was stealing from dealers in rich, south Regina,
Icepick, creamy bodyguard, smell of his hair.
Theurgist, he altered them into taking a collection
To hire a Detroit man to come and kill him;
Richard-Orpheus, him,
Waited for the man's plane to land
Then gored the man, and, as the man fell,
Kept rolling him through tarmac skirt gravel
With the whipping top of his head.

Richard's Thompson submachine
Gun under old meat in a cousin's porch freezer.

A party in north-central Regina
One evening, wolves
Moving up by the creek, swallows
Skimming grass in clicking ovals,
And this man, late in the festivities, late, cruised a knife into Richard's stomach.
They said it went way in. *Way* in.
Then the man went outside to sit in his car,
Light a smoke, passenger side,
Cosmonaut back from some difficult thing over the earth,
And Richard pulsed out
Of the house, over the lawn, knife still there,
Jiggling a bit,
And sent his hand through the side window
Throwing and throwing the voltage down
Into the face.
Is there not singing?

Richard blew cigarette smoke at houseflies
To calm them, then tied threads around their heads,
Looped these to each of his fingers and played
The strings like a piano appearing in air over his chrome table.
He sat once near the creek in a tree
And a book came onto his lap,
A book, flying over mild contours,
Over the plains and serially recited river systems,
Depths of snow, yet introspective this book,
Impossible to arrive, was coming to him,
Richard, coming to him, its smell of charring
Still on it, *The Mirror of Simple, Annihilated Souls and Those Who
Only Remain in Will and Desire of Love*, 1310, it was coming from June,
the book was coming from a square in Paris and that woman,
Standing inside the fire.
Marguerite Porete pushed out her book to Richard, his otter mouth,
As a boat for him, a flying power.

The Barracks, 1954

Paddy Lilburn speaks this

The government is bad so we live here
Half dug into a cliff of the End of Things,
Precipice of crowbelly cloud
And Serbian wolves, cliff
Comic and sheer and horsepowered
With history and top unseeable.
We used to live under bombs.
We live here now with *The Boy's Own
Paper*, reeking of ocean and hull, and wool
Socks drying on the radiator.
Walls of sheep skin colour of Ovaltine. Instead
Of meat curing on rods,
We have waiting.
The thicketed valleys speak only Cree,
The empire grows as proud flesh.
Our relatives and their children visit some nights
Coming through wreckage of snow in March
Between the cancer clinic and the cow barns,
Ice-rutted ways at their worst.
They may bring fruitcake or unpatchable jeans
And board games; their voices, heliumed,
Squeezed, are nearly, Raymond says, ours.
The herded walls at all hours inflate and empty
With the pneumatic force of contiguous families.
We are exactly nowhere.
There is something in the Name,
We read in the Gospel of John, that pushes
Glass-like, ideal objects from its very mouth,
And the world, this world now, bulbs,
We see, from even our speech.

Of

Hughie of wounds
Four or five years after the war, mortar shrapnel; they'd
Called his brother, my father, out of the lines in Italy
To consider what stirred in the pillow's cup;
Hughie and Ita, beautiful TB-ed London woman, they moved
To Vancouver in '46, then back to Liverpool, had a son named (I think)
Pat, still likely there if not himself dead – William Henry,
One-half or two-thirds gracious piece of apology,
Smelled of rain in hedges, Tullyglush,
Ednego, available as a beach landing craft just pushed up on, started out in the
British Army for reasons lost to me, taken at Dieppe, three years in camps,
Bacteria trail penmanship letters home, arthritis a second person
Gripping him to rise, too weak
To pull this off, though could stove
The surface of the first body –
Fred, first-born, of narcissism, maybe drink,
Drilled commandos in Vernon, he said, maybe so, a splashy
Knifeness about him, knifity – my father,
In charge, from Monte Cassino (Mt. John Cassian) on, of a tank,
Officer above him pared by a shell,
The war a small hotel in him, electrical fires in rooms 1, 3, and 5 –
Jack, on my mother's side, could have died
In Normandy, Holland, or any southeast Saskatchewan bar, heart,
Truck gliding into a ditch north of Corning, 1971,
Wheat delivered, licence renewed, beautiful,
Beautiful, their heavy-wind-in-poplar speeches,
Their sweeping movements in my half-lit, plush underage theatre; how they
Bent my breath.

II

Sara Riel, the Convent, Île-à-la-Crosse, 1874

A one-storey poplar pole building stands on a sandy point that juts into a large lake, canoes pulled up near. Two or three islands are visible in the distance, but not the other shore. She sits, enclouded in grey cloth, before a piano and speaks to her absent brother, who is in hiding, pursued by police in eastern Canada.

    I
This north takes me into its mouth, its lack
    of individuation a mouth, the unscrolling a mouth –
rivers, lakes, pines, tundra.
Pines, infinite lakes.
In the singing, children of Cree shale-
slipping up their voices' sides, I see fresh possibility,
fields growing edible bulbs, roads, creatures gnawing leaves,
the books of a new country, curled like baby mice inside the sound.
We could live there.
The plateau slightly below the peaks of what comes from their mouths.

My lungs first poured at that
particular hour winters back, two sloughs
slumped in me and I pooled in my bed,
upper parts of me dry enough
for elation-flares, conducting delivery of extreme unction. The priest said,
    pray to Marguerite-Marie Alacoque.
I did and forced the return of my clothes
which the sisters had ferociously hidden.
I bled and I lived and doubled my soul.
I returned to potato hills and the seeping mudroom.
I ought to bury my name
with my life under cemetery snow.
We eat only the lettuce
from mother's seeds,
the bed alive just inside the back door.

2
My eye falls
from the second world, smoking, but held
by a wire of loving is saved from water.
In this mobile, this monad with retractable green, paned wings
I have my own homunculous equipment.
I smell the action of chlorophyll
and it noses me
and thus I see the skeleton of language
inside deer's bodies and inside pike's
swim paths. I read it
meaning it hums at me and around me.
Oratio pro lacrimus. I would
be the food of my tears.
I did not make a bid on Rupert's Land.
I was not a signatory to Treaty 6.
I gather voices escaping
from all things produced as matter,
harvesting them as I would wild rice,
gently tapping along their sides.

End of August

Queen Anne's lace, lurk
of vetch in forests, white
clover shaken in a fist of final bees,
dust chalks everywhere.
And the gloom of fireweed
in abandoned quarries,
autumn's vampiric looks;
a leaf falls from oceanspray,
this is thinking.
A dog barks,
cold pours its slag
       in a scoop through sky.

The hoard of neglect
is in the beauty-vault of things.
Fewer than eight red pear leaves
among sodden pine needles on my low shed roof.

Swan Plain

I've found the place.
This is what I've decided.
Couple of trailers, a store
From the party days in the early Fifties at the crossroads,
Some chocolate bars inside, whitening, four
Or five packs of cigarettes, Export "A," devices for dehorning cattle.
I fall to pieces, Patsy Cline.
You can feel it, soaked into everything,
Palatial entropy.
I'd move the Vatican here
Or something like Pythagoras's camp.
A few aluminum lawn chairs on the grassy carpet
Between the units: the curia.
Lovely place for it. Juan, the Card (aka primo
Cardinale), in one of the single-wides. Marcel, holographic
Archbishop of Axel Heiberg Island, also there. If you needed more
Shopping, there's always the town
Of Plenty near. We'd quietly lay down
The *anathema sit*s over a few beers after supper, waving away mosquitoes,
Taking turns tipping poplar chunks into the firepit.
The beckoning of this is heading in our direction.
Allan Stanley moved the puck behind the net and looked up.
The moment clicking, engine shedding heat.
This is how it works out.
Everything will be padded in and fine.

Oh

Living in the truck west
of Lake Cowichan, past the Youbou turn,
almost at the coast,
in the bloom of sleeping
bag and charcoal, back quiet in thin valleys,
walking, poking around with a stick, in clear-cut, in slash,
I am one of the first to meet winter coming
off the great water
and give it my name, which disappears
inside.
Étienne Gilson on Bernard's mystical theology,
book of lips and breath,
top maps, I soft-mouthed exegete, parking receipts, one
black banana on the dash, another on the passenger-side floor.
Coho just beginning to taste
the freshwater fan
at the tip of the creeks,
eagles slide three hundred miles toward rivers' emptying mouths.
I slot whatever else I have to say into reed-shuffle at Lizard Lake.
Cold flows off the morning moon,
oak leaves turning purple-black
at the foot of southern mountains.

Tim Lilburn the trained Jesuit seal has for years etc.

The mountain's take-no-prisoners hump,
seen from the second-floor window
of the X-ray clinic, over late-day traffic,
sickens me, a lightness that goes all
the way in.
Just above traffic, gravelly air,
                            a sluggish creek.
These dismemberments, which, it is
said, are leaves falling, the wind shifting.
The mountain puts strangeness sickness on me
untranslatable to prednisone.
Here its 9,000-year-old name
in SENĆOTEN I have in a tight winding of light,
the hard tip of our relations. Day by day
I look at the mountain and walk and groom it (tearing out
ivy and Scotch broom) and think in a small, single-occupant
craft toward the middle of its galactic mass
where I believe the will to sit across a minute cocktail table
from me in a film from the early 1940s
and receive looks from me through its drinking face
exists, cleaning its paws.
I would bitch at it and deliciously
gossip and cook up schemes.
This morning I considered the hideous gravity –
swift black timing chain in necessity's
machine churning through objects' teeth – was the real visage
of the beautiful friend.
Yes, but how then breathe?

Fucked Up, All Fucked Up

the weather wrote again
John Newlove

And snow clouds rode by your mansion
heart, where you kept a few rooms, some blankets,
a hot plate, but it's always been panic
and geography for me, so I feed myself
into the art of driving
up the eastern coast on this island, into and out of washed-sheer,
one-storey towns shaken out in blown sand
and mountain shadow,
secretive and weakened
by, say, the murder of a striking miner, 1910,
whose name appears on a plaque outside the pickle-smelling
museum: the miner stops, grows mountainous
but the towns blur forward, thinning,
loosening at the core, winter-closed shop selling fudge,
bankrupt day spa – people, irresponsible people,
say I have a mental disease,
a wolf inside, smoking, I see and cry at; and thus I drive much farther
north into the forests and isolate peaks
        of the far north island,
cut blocks and commercial fishing boats
that ting in the ruff of the killing sea,
far northern, incoherent towns stubbed in by absent-
minded fir and, feeling around, locate no psychagogic slack,
no golden thread or the Vast Earth,
or even actual, rapt stoppage in trees, valley Vs or swamps,
the eye cogged to Cat treads, or the eye's acreage
in the frontal cortex pricklingly lit by true and untrue RCMP
helicopters scouting marijuana plantations along dried gorges.
And the road falls apart into
gravel past Port Hardy, curving to the west side

of the north island, the stare of that place power-washed of affect
by wind, nothing-thereness, flowing rock; amoebic
hamlets lie jammed at the end of long inlets reachable by boat
                                    after January storms,
homesteads on footings of disability pensions
and massive flat screens,
driving into that as a breathing,
as the voice of the Zurich-seminared analyst,
as anonymous, general pleading I paddle
with the assist of, want like Value Village sweaters
cargoing the smell of many of us I go in the power of, to see
a way to myself clear.

Magnus es, Domine, et laudabilis valde (**Augustine,** *Confessions*)

The animals orbit, elk, flickers,
moose, one white tail with the face of St. Rose of Lima,
as thick moons
both above grass and against a heavy muscle slab
inside hills, their looks shafts.
The eyes grown by the flanks of the most eastern hills
pour their oddly odoured light into the animals' eyes
so an isthmus inches between them, vital drip, breath
tube, and this luscious, communicated paste secures, *binds up*,
the tangled elliptical rushes of creatures.

Exempla

    1

Someone has returned from the dead
Wearing a stone-weighted blue coat that falls to his toes,
Illuminated with equations and nouns in Arabic and Latin
Stitched in white thread along its arms, both the tops
And under, and from the shoulders to the knee.
The words and numbers slant and cross each other
On the outside and up and down the inner lining.
When he fully opens the panes of this coat,
You see fire moving in a circular current
On his body, uptaking fuel of his smell,
Downward toward his feet then into grass
And into wet ground where it begins
A sleepy lunge and touches him again, falling
Along both sides of his head.
Clinkers arc from this fire and perforate
The hands of anyone watching.

    2

The young man has seen something
And refuses to speak.
He hides in the wounds of the mountain,
Its gorings
And won't come down below the snow to calls.
He saw the man standing in the choir,
Blood fountaining from his eyes and ears.
The young man's complete body shook in the act
Of hearing at that moment.
It whipped in the taste, a single alert organ.
The curl of blond ash bucked
From the cross and pinned him between its arms.

Below he sees the tips of pines move and notes
The smell coming off snow.

    3
In the room of Selo of Wilton, the shield comes
Out of curtains of dark and reflects
The late-twelfth-century face
Of the syllogistic master at Oxford.
In the midst of the gruff glow
Of the nubbly surface, just before the reflected face, a mouth
Floats from the metal and speaks
Through the layer of the face
In the room's frost.
Master Selo's time is short, his years vain.
A fire burns, snapping in the room.
The master's dead student, nude, appeared
Two nights ago, with even his skin removed
By the whip of thin weapons.
Lipless, he quivered in hatred
Of argument.
No one tonight holds the shield that cups
The soft candle of the teacher's face.
Here is the spur of true philosophy.
Ether stirs in the room, a throaty wisp,
As the metal thing passes through it.

Black Hut

The black hut, outlined in blue, the voice,
Backs into the forest, Gershom Scholem's
Major Trends rides its desk,
Floating, abetting the dream unit.
Snow has only just disappeared. Exhausted light,
Light that's come through surgery and its superb
Mini-bar of morphine, coils in the window,
Tough, or obsessed, strand Clerk Maxwell's
Displacement current egged, pished, straightforwardly
Begged to stipple in nothing. It's here and loaded.
The fruitless pear tree near bloom in cold
Grows an inch forward, first moments
Of originary inflation replayed. One of its branches
Rakes the roof.
Adonis says, *The innards of matter come toward me.*
They do, they walk as if they knew
The body they moved in was Hector Berlioz's
Symphonie Fantastique, Leonard Bernstein's version, 1968. Or
The True Spirit and Original Intent of Treaty 7.

Rabbit Lake Log House, Where I First Read the *Tao*

Stove of quarter-inch iron
In a wide grey room facing the opposite
Plunge of the valley, frost on the inner walls, the early Nineties –
Where else to sleep but in front of that cherried blackness,
One sleigh, drifts, and a moon pressed into the metal,
In a winter bag, on a moose-hide rug, waking every few hours
To lay in poplar chunks broken
From the iced pile behind the kitchen.
I'd light a propane lamp later,
Put a kettle on the hottest part of the stove's plate
For instant and watch white trees come out of dark.
A beautiful woman had left me.
Unskinned stars every night,
The river was frozen a half-mile below
Under animal scratches through snow.
The house was still and stepped back even in late morning,
Horsehair couch, some sort of tiptoedness in the biblical quotations
In glass ovals on the wall; the old logs in the loaned house
Cracked as if they made a boat
Moving across a sea of buoyant cold.

Nature

I am trying to read the form of longing
And see a wind with the sun inside it
Coming out of the east, 6:45 a.m.,
Moving across the campus where I have a room
For a few days, in the south part of the city,
Near the ring road and flooded fields past that.
A small moon earlier, around five,
In a fog of distance, over mowed grass in the quadrangle.

All conscious life (says the *Summa
Contra Gentiles*) streams to throw its bright rope
Around the torso of God, or seeds
In the mind of God or the necks
Of dolphins in the mind of God.

960 Garnet, the aunts, uncles, parents
Sitting around two card tables, late
In the Fifties, tumblers of rye and ginger,
Eating bridge mix, Planters nuts,
Cards expertly shuffled and dealt.
All with cigarettes, unfiltered, maybe menthol,
The men in jackets, one without in braces and shirt band,
All in shined shoes, the women in nylons.
Their laughter whippy with sexual crest,
They wave their cigarettes as they argue
Their hands and tease and quickly,
Now and then, like birds feeding, touch one another,
Shoulders and wrists.
Around midnight the women bring out
Lunch – sandwiches, coffee, fruitcake – as if
Beating another thin wall of gold
To one already there.

The winter outside, monstrously wide
Ford engine blocks sink and clot in frost.
There is a carefully flaked and notched
Brown flint point from the Avonlea Culture
Lost under three layers of gloaming
In air near them, then a little farther on,
A chip of corded, grey pottery from the Old Woman's Culture
Lies on its side on a slope of some brilliant tilth.
They wave their cigarettes in the air's gold churn,
Kids ducking under the swooping ember blobs,
Shoot back their heads, showing teeth, and howl.

III

The Munroe Wing

Dwayne, out, decomposing rapidly under his layers, moves
This oversized, dragging parka through mounded streets
To snare diamond services from the city's most mephistopholean
Lawyer who'll collect for him,
Singular him, his own gorgeous death benefits.
Soon, soon, he writes back.
Demons tear out like rusted spikes
Or reseat themselves with chaffs and nudges almost soundlessly
In Greenlandish fluorescense on floors above.
Reskind uncovers his wrist tattoo, its blue leaps on me,
Poultice, a pure alchemical coat, to haul what sickness I hide
To the edge of my skin where it can be scraped
Like foam from boiling potato water.
The white of their coats could pare corns.
The girlfriend contrives to come, but moves in
A surf of curling walls.
My razor, however, relishes its quarantine in the nursing station,
Below their starchings. The blade across my jaw
Has become a spectator sport and draws crowds.
Out around the edge-of-town slum, I kicked
My great-uncle's Meteor's sullen-to-be-matter fixity
Into a sweat until it flew or turned into the farthest pitch
Of the human voice, so had to lay the keys across the caseworker's palm.
I grew a hump
And learned my place among stone and chokecherry.
Dwayne'd meet me in cafés after I got out
To go over his plans, complicated as physics
Of the hypostatic union, how he'd play it
When the sky descended for him. But mostly he fretted
About his small white dog, big as a slipper, whose sweet, girlish name
I heard as "anomie."
Back and forth on the pavement, our stopped, flash faces.

The Fifties

By the creeks, shacks warmed by heaving –
The walls reek of muskrat –
Quebec heaters, nothing
But wood shavings between the studs, kids
Pale as posts inside and outside in slack
Rubbed-through coats, rabbit weed skin or frog spawn
Of homes near the seepage of Duck's farm.
They'd keep us in at recess
To glug goat's milk, greyness and slap in the taste.
Ringworm in shared hockey gloves.
The immense stamina of the Fifties everywhere in air,
Parka-ed workers under tons of small stones in northern bunkers
Funnelling nosecone plutonium.
Sweeney's lowered, piggy eyelashes,
The abandoned silence of his skin, which he sucked quarter-inch
By quarter-inch deeper,
As we yelled at him and the teacher yelled, into his torso and face,
He eating.
He thus had a dirty, pink-eyed light.

Surely Wilfred's towering instant was
When he robbed the nightclub
Under the bank, emptying one barrel of his shotgun
Into the vermiculite ceiling,
Him descending through
The whallop of dust and its numb drift.
Petite, blond, small-mouthed, easily shivable
Once he turned up at the Prince Albert Penitentiary,
Where a glow
No bigger than an adult's palm
In its own circle of float,
A little island

Sucked at his eye.
The Great Béguinage of Paris, 1305,
What had become of it, I recognize it, women entering
And leaving the walls,
A fluid emptiness lizarding up
Throughout them, the walking and sitting women
In the miniature city in the jail air,
While at that moment it also flared, such bright, persistent nothing,
And settled on all our mothers' hair.

Deer Place Hut

What a long walk back
to it and who
knows the dialect?
The animals pool there.
A line of ice above us
adds an inch down
and the room's light grows
greener, atoms tighter.
Lean over *The Great Code*
where it lies in the rot on the desk,
as if hatcheting in crows and flickers
on the west side of the mountain, all raccoons,
deer were welling
above it, the very book,
lumpy, spiking look cross-hairing, lodged, over
the writing in the book. Truly have
to clean this desk.
Ricorso – but in one late, late,
scene in eros's mystagogia, opera, clever,
sad, foot-careful, they muster
before the odour of this alone-ity, the room that is a room-
coat, the smell of theatre screen lightly
cooked by images,
mostly of our small, shapely wills moving their hands.
A line of ice, ascesis and fate, forms above us
brush of pear branch on this mossed roof.

That Time

Clearing boxes in the evening
pickup, sometime near the middle of June,
driving a worn-to-pink red International Harvester van
contracted to the post office, nothing
holding but my arm the engine cowling
in place, stick shift jumping
from the exposed gear mesh when I rise
into second, I was quick,
out of the cab, key the box, scoop mail into the flop of the bag,
again and again through curving suburbs, northwest Regina,
right out to fields of canola.
I'd cut back on drinking and was reading Gurdjieff,
played like a pickerel by thinking, thinking, psychiatrized (when did I
 expect to see
transparent burning angels walking six feet above the world?) and he'd, G,
mentioned Mt. Athos, brief camp there, the monks in their phone booth
  stone rooms,
them news to me Europe had such a thing
and in weeks, probably, I was seven leagues in John of the Cross,
then Richard Rolle, and by mid-August, circling *The Cloud*,
had caught in myself the stag, the wanted animal, lifting its nose to water.
When it came, it was like melting and choral singing
going on just inside the skin.
Flashing tears were drinking me.
Ruusbroec says this will or kiss is bulimic, it
eats, it eats you down.
It hit me mostly in the face that early evening,
subcuticle wind that was the torso of Christ,
low light between the houses, kids in the street on bicycles,
lilacs with their heavy leaves,
then it worked a way into my neck.
The truck moving south in the last few streets before the creek,

passing in front of the house my parents bought two years later.
I slept on the floor the rest of the summer,
my belt tightened hard around my chest.

Poem Coming to Ruusbroec

Nine thousand gallons of gasoline slide
    from a gashed tanker into Goldstream salmon creek
and finish coho smelt and shellfish in the first ten minutes. Ferns
at the waterfall two miles, mostly
vertical, from the mouth of the creek
at Finlayson Arm, flick in updraft.
The drunk driver, dragging a fifty-five-foot tank
and pup, is believed, carving his rig along the rock,
to be not impaired but in performance in a theatre
with wicked prongs to pry Tsartlip First Nation from
the east bank on nonceded land.

The third line NHL centre (retired),
worst player ever to wear the sacred number 9, an
embarrassment, condo-izing from the west over
Skirt Mountain toward the water, gets this and that.
People talk about John Bolenbaugh
taking a head-kicking and tires slashed for complaining
about the non-existent Enbridge cleanup
last summer in Michigan.
Dog capital plants its nose in this anus then that.
Splits of sun between alders. Ruusbroec
could occupy a house made from this veneer,
its foundation slightly above his left shoulder.
The moss stinks, the underwater stones stink,
the rootballs of alders and salal slick with the dead meat of gasoline.
I'd see fifteen-pound carcasses,
hundreds, eggs tailed a while back into gravel, on both sides of the water,
each November I've been here, eagles
too fat to fly, biomass weighed in tons – all done
for two runs at least.

A cougar comes through two days later,
out of the Malahat Hills, not hunting, moving slowly,
late in the morning, and shows
itself, working its soft shoulders behind a crowd
of journalists turned to ask the stream biologist
something. She stares at the cat, the only one she's ever seen.
People four generations back called the salmon
that came in the spring, first new food
after winter, the pitiful ones, flipping
matters in their piety and end-of-the-rains wreckage, they,
themselves, understanding they were write-offs
if the big fish didn't turn up.
Two years out in the north Pacific,
carried on the tremble of electromagnetic musk,
they tumble in, fat, skittering.

A poplar blooms on the other, drier side
of the Rocky Mountains, in front of the hotel
at the arts centre, where poets stay and sleep and think
and put down phrases. The poplar opens
like the Pantokrator. Just after Easter. Roads
closed from snow.
This is where the stag showed me by its nostrils
one night the way below things. I ended up in the hospital ten days later,
riding the horns of a medieval infection. The mountain on which the deer
stood is, or at least was then, a reborn Waldensian,
as far as I could make out, but we can
                          wink at this. Another story.
Now we go to Groenendaal, the green valley,
1359, which is where the poem has wanted
to be for a while, John Ruusbroec, Flemish, celibate, sits under a tree,
canon regular, with his stylus and wax tablet, in the community's
farthest field. The names
below the names of everything here

could come forward,
glossy and undulant as otters.
He has read in the book *Sister Catherine*
                    the nun say,
"Sir, rejoice with me. I have become God."
And this has laid a bone in his throat, her auditor
believed to be Meister Eckhart, and R. wants to work
out how union is not identity, and so get this logarithm
out of his nose, the funeral home floral smell
of its romance.
He works in the paradise of the wound of the saviour
in that verdant valley of thickly gathering
tastes. He works the work
of the mouth of the inside and
the mansions of the palate and he works
the spread of the cupped, lusciously textured, hidden-in-
a-rolled-leaf ear, its mechanism and splendour-drinking,
silver, quivering ingestion: he gathers
the wind and radio tangles of
tongueable sound, the sound that goes
under the tongue.
In the green land.
There are streams of honey at this moment under the
            human garden skin,
a sold-out football stadium of possible
tastes, all activated.
You sit among these
and overcome the world,
in the spray of the meadow, which is
the precise seepage of dilation.
Union without identity he sees
Is the necessity of ethics and love.

Summer, 1971

I am extracted
and soon enjoy
becoming exhaust
along the screw of the tongue,
the pulleys of sugar.
There was a sheet descending of the thought
of melting.
I am in a postal truck, clearing boxes close to supper,
tipping and rolling within
in the current of speaking and speaking the Jesus prayer.
On the bank
of this voice,
my Tullyglush Irish grandmother,
peppermints in her apron pockets,
knuckly protestant stare
(red mushroom pushing up at her feet),
criminally slips mints to the spaniel.
She's the one on the bank of this speaking.
Sugar arc. I know it.
I was slipped envelopes
containing the meats of light,
the sweat of the lintel and the frame were sent
to soak into me.

The Leighton Ford Crusade, Regina Exhibition Stadium, 1962

August, the bleachers are packed, you can still smell hockey equipment
From the Pats season, the last home game,
As well as hay from Agribition and the bull sale.
Tight, concussing heat in the gravel parking lot
But a cool, furry duskiness even in the seats below the rafters.
The stage is lit hard,
Full of handsome Americans in suits, snakes in their fists,
Protruding from their mouths, or fountaining from their groins,
And him in his blond forties and the local choir.
The first combines dip into fields,
Clang and snick of cutting teeth,
Moan of grain passing through the machines beyond the edges of town.
The robes of the choir shake and exhale as the mass rises.
Postal workers, housewives, men in love with seals, bagpipers, they rise.
Falling wheat and the robes – the utter autonomy of nature.
At the last hymn I go over the boards
Where the red line must have been, and walk on sailcloth
Over planks above the black oval where the ice was
                toward the pulsing front.
In the wheat, grasshoppers arc just before the combine's paddles
Slice down.
The clothes of the thousands and the light
Of the stage jerk in a miniscule breeze.
Creeks are rolling off mountains
Along my arms and hips, and my feet seem to stride on them
Down the generous aisle, I weighing more,
Greatly more and also less than minutes before.

IV

Rivers and Mountains in the Mouth of the Exegetical Choir

Coastal thunder, early July, mustering, pre-Feast of Benedict, just before
        dawn, in pre-birds dark, rare, yet
Starting pistol for TEKI to slash
Into silt curtain, tree tusk lattice, the odd spring
        salmon carried in the rivers' load, luminous family,
collected in one of the river's turning sacs. Long grass idles to the sea.
Cat with a new rabbit, squealing, in her mouth
Runs along the side of the white stucco house,
Black cat, small, collarless, living under the cliff.
Coastal thunder, rare, just before dawn.
Thunder's freight – nitrogen enters garden soil, dragon-enters
Used iris soil,
And where camus have produced anthracite seeds.
The black roll from one side of the valley
To the other, a wrecked knee tipping to the lip of its socket
Then settling back.
The cat, a Montanist, is the crest
        of a side-channel dialectical roll, Spirit's roll.
Lore moves in cedar trunks ("to
        unseal the soul   to untie the knots
               that bind it" (Abraham Abulafia)),
Each thing interprets and unleashes the other,
Intellectus agens, common electrochemical carry, leaps through the forms.

Morning forest, north slope of P,KOLS,
        the smell, fir sap, Oregon grape,
Light through Douglas fir, cedar,
Is the smell out of which soil, mind
And rain rolls and passes over.
Two fawns in the yard, weened, under the not-
in-the-greatest-shape rose, doe appearing every few days.

In the shed Zhai Yongming's *The Changing Room*, "another kind of skin,"
        presses down on the desk.
The bigger fawn later materializes
                out of 9:00 a.m. ridge sun, cliff
In shadow.

Retreat

When I was on Salt Spring Island, hiding out beside that lake,
its dawns and geese and small ice, reading Marguerite Porete, it was so cold
I had to leave the oven door open
and pull the kitchen table up beside it.
I climbed in the late afternoon, trails that went straight up, no hesitation.
Also I was tucking into Jerome Rothenberg reporting on Robert Duncan,
his massed parliaments of pretty well everything. The NHL quarter finals
were on and the Vancouver Canucks
were being slowly taken apart, beginning with the multi-millionaire goalie.
That woman, fire swimming around
her, her book that brought fire to her
beautiful and shocking as a sandhill crane.
The prelates generously warned her, they, the people they sent, burned her
book in front of her three years before the day
of the larger fire in the Paris square. She said nothing to any of them.

Snow, remarkable snow, in the branches of a large-leaf maple,
remarkable for this month and here,
crows landing, snow puffing up
at the impact of the black feet.

Feast

Scrape of moon on dogwood leaves and
on blue cliff stone,
full moon, so far away as to be the moon
of some future life, bright, gelid glow
around 5:30 a.m., feast of Thérèse
(Martin) of Lisieux, mother dead at five,
four sisters not making adulthood,
her small, boxed face, that wimpled moon, tuberculosis.
The tomatoes we've hauled out of the garden
in sacks these last weeks, seven inches, some, across,
none split. Bag after bag.
Cat food sodden in the dish at the back door after rain.
Next night a demon wind licks through
and just before dawn,
one giant maple leaf sways above the deck
in a torn spiderweb. This now is the Feast
of the Guardian Angels, whose mouths
are wound over our minds,
warming individual letters of their alphabet
and ours, which then wake in us and move.

Against "Linguistic Fragmentation as Political Intervention in Calgarian Poetry," derek beaulieu, *Open Letter*, Summer, 2008

a nod to Barry McKinnon

Rolling, weather on its gigantic, flanged wheels, Rolling,
uncurling, then curling, over clefts feeding into the Nass, heaving
over snowfields and buttes north of
Dawson Creek, the Athabasca and over
the fuse of the South Saskatchewan and Red Deer, over grain and over
that again, over horse
flats south of Mankota, the secrecy of things, the jump of Cree
        uttered in night alleys and Portage Ave.
music, the theatre of armed robbery on 11th Avenue, Regina, rolling,
back down the Assiniboine and up then into trees and rivers north, the whole
of the Hudson Bay sale (1869),
the operatic stealing that staggered Big Bear with its wingspread and augered
money into settlers' wagons and throats after WWI and after that, growing
wheat, wheat, wheat, wheat,
wheat and the land sinking and growing
coal-bed methane and sour wells.

I dreamt people swim-flying
        horizontally four feet under the ground.
I dream the gears and proteins
        of angling downward into the earth
and back with a word like a knife or
        grass seed in my mouth.
I dreamt the regency of pumpkins.
I dreamt the horse dance and feather-show of Riel's theophany.
I dreamt water.
I dreamt a non-autocratic
        Catholicism, Ibn 'Arabian angels agent intellectly lowering it on a bed
sheet, their bright ankles. I dreamt a coffee date with John Ruusbroec.

So now we come back to what we walk on and can't
know. The poetics of disgust
is used, as you say, as a hammer is used against the Victorian and NASA
fuselage and armoire of capital, but at strike point
slops apart into a fleshy danglement or an open mouth
to the device, not, armed, serving cake but presenting a fretted edge
to the duvet in the bourgeois bedroom.
I put my mouth against the forest duff
and wait. (I've been pulling ivy on the west side of Mt. Tolmie)
I put my mouth against the forest floor and wait.

But here is something better.
Now I will bring waters and wires
from Proclus's throat and draw and affix these
to the poem's mouth
>   *What other reason*
>   *can we give for the fact that the heliotrope follows in its movement*
>   *the movement of the sun and the selenotrope for the movement of the*
>   *moon, forming a procession within the limits of their power,*
>   *behind the torches of the universe*

Rolling, rolling, cleating down, the unfolding
eye, its weather, joying out a craft, talk and looking mobile, over Lake
Lenore, Wolverine Creek, Pelican Point on
Last Mountain Lake, over reeds, the town
of Craven, we undergo this into the act of initiation into interpretation,
and into the Qu'Appelle River west of Piapot First Nation.

And Proclus wells out of air again.
>   *For in truth each thing prays*
>   *according to the rank it occupies in nature, and sings*
>   *the praise of the leader of the divine series to which it belongs,*

a spiritual or rational or physical or sensual praise; for the heliotrope
moves to the extent that it is free to move, and in its rotation, if we could hear
the sound of the air buffeted by its movement

Rolling, Proclus listening to the play of the plant and speaking
Treatise on the Hieratic Art of the Greeks, which I put against
The Victoria *Times Colonist* and alongside *I Wanted to Say*
Something and *Wood Mountain Poems*, Proclus the long-feathered,
Proclus the lone horse moving south of Rockglen, Saskatchewan.

we should be aware that it is a hymn
to its king, such as it is within the power of a plant to sing.

P,KOLS Song Cycle

Half-words

The language appears as a boat
brushing through ten-day-rain trees.
We can see it through smoke or fog tail,
boat of human and animal hair, on closer
examination, and tree hair and brindled
mushrooms,
old or burnt hair boat smell the language,
SENĆOŦEN the boat, tongue, mouth-hover, of the tidal region,
its last glaciation nouns, tarred with pliable rhythms
of the mouth, undertongue *uush uush* sound,
spongy glottal click.
It appears in multiple versions, mouth-boats, and in
each a bulb-naked human, 1.5 metres
high with a cranial ridge, our most trustworthy,
on some points, minds.
Each of these is lightning-shoved and dead-dropped by her nakedness,
that is, a lack of stratospheric protection, so everything
lances them and this hurt, power
flaring out, existentiates almost entirely the boats
that move through the trees.
All hear the *whiff* and *whuff*
of the tiny keels tottering
through northern rainforest,
each boat nosing very slowly among trees,
not too high, on the mountain's west sharp slope.
They call to one another the small
otherwise quiet beings at the stern oars
softly and with mere half-
word sounds and raccoons,
madrones, ferns, chanterelles

angle toward them,
allowing a slight splaying
to come into their own dear selves.

Epithalamion

My brother and I, Greg and I, spent some weeks
waiting under the creek, Wascana Creek, when we were ten or eleven.
We found various ways to breathe.
We were in unroaded parts then in that place
of unmarried muskrats, avocets,
and we worked toward the pure heart, alert *polis*, with the muskrats though
we had little idea of what was up, sex at this point a certain
edge instability, and toward algae and reeds,
frogs and the rot smell in mud.
These all kept our names.

Our mother called us in,
Fireflies swam us out after supper to the Pelletiers, running
in dusk.
We'd wandered into a place of no-Christian roads
and took part, as we anticipated, in play marriages
with one creek bend, one muskrat we'd killed and others,
dogs and sage, which ended badly or
just stopped.
So those summers around the fleshy weeds.

Now I am here. The shed
– walled garden – is a hump behind the head
of a woolly rhinoceros, middle Paleolithic. I live almost entirely
in this fatty palace.
It hurtles in one dimension but
on the matter of intention observes
radio silence.

Some mornings star
embers, then later rain.

Wind, Weighed in the Cables

Ashy or Tuareg-blue spreading
webs, while, behind,
a hundred nailheads of crows
cluster in oaks and Douglas fir,
bunches of sunk quills.
Flickers, wing-fanning, brush the mountain's
west side;
webs like drums
blooded with dew,
drum quiver, the web's
hand drum
almost throat-closed with dew in fog,
lilac to eave and cedar hedge
tip to a point, yes?, high
right, not there – air's noumenon, nothing
but providential docking, sly ingress;
the spider a moving knuckle,
jerky, brown intelligence,
needling legs, the waddle.
A hissing rush comes
from the water around the peninsula as a salmonoid
wind, early November, passes through it.

Error

The crow swallows the cat's pellets on the back deck
whole as it would fingers on a battlefield,
coins in an axe-opened chest.
Crows dark rivets on a slow arcing bridge.

The names float in the gnostic
rings and in physis's slurry.
W̱MIEŦEN, P,KOLS, asphalted Bowker Creek, west
side of P,KOLS, Cordova Bay, T̲IQENEN̲, rain pocking leaf pools,
drainage ditches running, sword fern.
The meal-serving names, bed-providing
names in the old language, circling in their gnostic rings.
Rain pushes out from shore slowly
like hunched riders or people climbing
into quiet's nests in Garry Oaks.
Crows dark as rivets on the long bridge.

The crow's feet, sooty chains,
beat the deck's white-painted metal railing
above the cat's mouse-decalled bowl.
How the crow flails the metal,
entropy, error,
and then looks up at us from below,
tips his head and looks from beneath,
Eleusinian eye,
and behind this frisking, nothing is quiet,
mossed stone in dry stacked walls,
cedar frond, sticks, pulled-down
nailholes in old 2x4s, golf balls
ironed from the parking lot at the mountain's
scenic lookout, lying in decayed leaves,
feint and compose themselves,
feeling for a seam to massively infiltrate,
the interest inside things
in us, rising like a scent.

Hummingbird

a curdling in rain
heated by its own stony force
to a coaly roux,
stretch of turbulence in
the downward spearing
winter creek: a hummingbird
gathers flesh behind fuchsia
before the Douglas firs' frozen wall.
in the bird's helmeted look
my face is an inner-dimpling tunnel
moving, touched
by the whipped ends of yellow grass.
spiderweb lanks clotted with a slanting
daemon attending *me*, haloed full body
with metabolic fever,
trouble in middle air, the bird, erupts
on air's skin,
smudge or blear in the black
from the door in the morning trees,
attack-fountaining the bird, stupendously
visioned speed.

Mountain

The winds' faces go into the rise
Behind me and don't come out.
There are heads, necks, and faces in there.
Moonlight's grind against earth,
5:00 a.m., produces dust
Detectable on the tongue, exhaust
From moving circularity.
The pear tree arcing over the shed
Still compressed by the weight of this light hours after.
I put my finger along it to gauge its thickness.
I am in exile.
Ibn 'Arabi, says Corbin, saw the *huwiya*,
Divine ipseity, as the Arabic letter *ha*,
Suffused, scarved with sun, placed on a red carpet;
"Between the two branches of the *ha* gleam the letters *hw* (*huwa*,
He), while the *ha* projects its rays upon four spheres."
Idle pear tree.
The shed rolls forward
Each corner on the heave of a warm back.

Notes and Acknowledgements

Poems in this collection have previously appeared in *CV2*, *Vallum*, *Lake*, *Canadian Poetries*, and the anthologies *Islands or Continents* (Hong Kong) and *Tag: Canadian Poets at Play*. Some were gathered, with Mandarin translations, in the chapbooks "Newton, Force at a Distance, Imperialism" (Chinese University of Hong Kong Press and Columbia University Press, 2014) and "The Rabbit Lake Log House Where I First Read the Tao" (Minsheng Art Museum, trans. Huang Canran, Shanghai, 2015).

I thank Ken Babstock for his help with final edits. And I thank Kevin Paul for his SENĆOŦEN instruction.